GRAPHIC SCIENCE

UNDERSTANDING

GLOBAL WARMING

WITH MAX AXIOM
SUPER SCIENTIST

by Agnieszka Biskup

illustrated by Cynthia Martin and Bill Anderson

Consultant:
Joseph M. Moran, PhD
Associate Director, Education Program
American Meteorological Society, Washington, D.C.

Capstone press

Mankato, Minnesota

Graphic Library is published by Capstone Press,
151 Good Counsel Drive, P.O. Box 669, Mankato, Minnesota 56002.
www.capstonepress.com

1  2  3  4  5  6  12  11 10  09  08  07

*Library of Congress Cataloging-in-Publication Data*
Biskup, Agnieszka.
    Understanding global warming with Max Axiom, super scientist / by Agnieszka Biskup;
illustrated by Cynthia Martin and Bill Anderson.
    p. cm.—(Graphic library. Graphic science)
    Summary: "In graphic novel format, follows the adventures of Max Axiom as he
explains the science behind global warming"—Provided by publisher.
    Includes bibliographical references and index.
    ISBN-13: 978-1-4296-0139-9 (hardcover)
    ISBN-10: 1-4296-0139-6 (hardcover)
    1. Global warming—Juvenile literature. 2. Adventure stories—Juvenile literature. I.
Martin, Cynthia, 1961– ill. II. Anderson, Bill, 1963– ill. III. Title. IV. Series.
    QC981.8.G56B525 2008
    363.738'74—dc22                                                     2007002269

*Art Director and Designer*
Bob Lentz

*Cover Artist*
Tod Smith

*Colorist*
Krista Ward

*Editor*
Christopher L. Harbo

Photo illustration credits: NASA, 15; Shutterstock/Margaud, 21

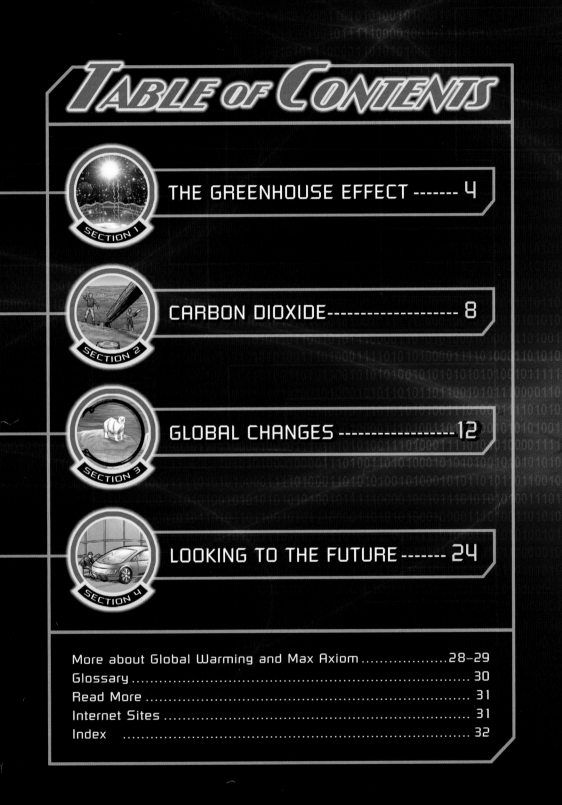

# TABLE of CONTENTS

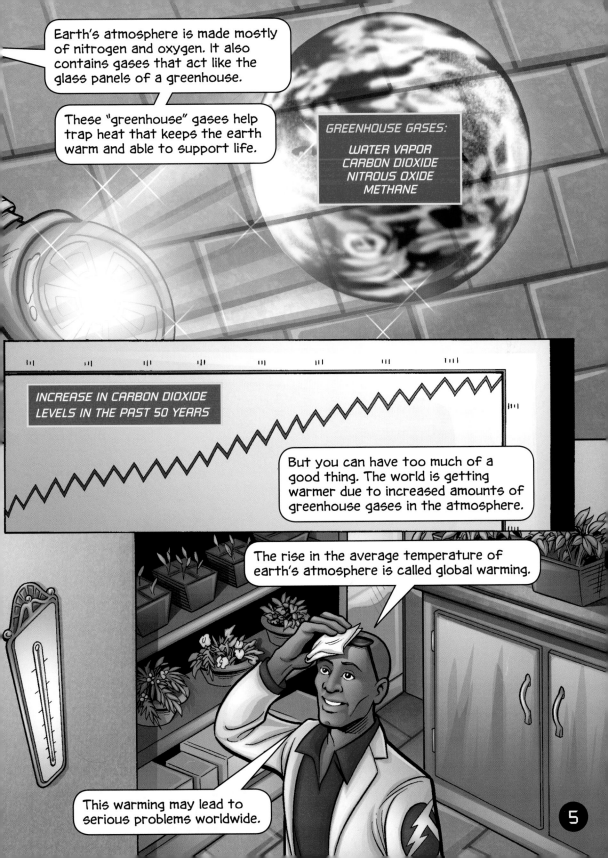

Let's take a closer look at how the greenhouse effect works.

Our atmosphere allows the sun's rays to warm the earth's surface.

Heat from the earth is then radiated out into space.

SUNLIGHT

RADIATED HEAT

RADIATED HEAT

But some heat is also absorbed by greenhouse gases and radiated back to earth. Without the greenhouse effect, the earth would be too cold for most forms of life.

## HOT AND COLD MOON

The moon has no atmosphere. Its equator is a blistering 260 degrees Fahrenheit (127 degrees Celsius) in daylight. In darkness the temperature drops to a frigid minus 280 degrees Fahrenheit (minus 173 degrees Celsius).

But the amount of some gases, especially carbon dioxide, has been rising. More greenhouse gases mean more heat is being radiated back to earth. The result is a warmer planet.

RADIATED HEAT

Scientists believe human activities are the reason there's more carbon dioxide in the air.

HYBRID

Car exhaust, for example, contains carbon dioxide. One hundred years ago, very few cars traveled our roads.

Today, they clog our highways and release tons of carbon dioxide into the air every day.

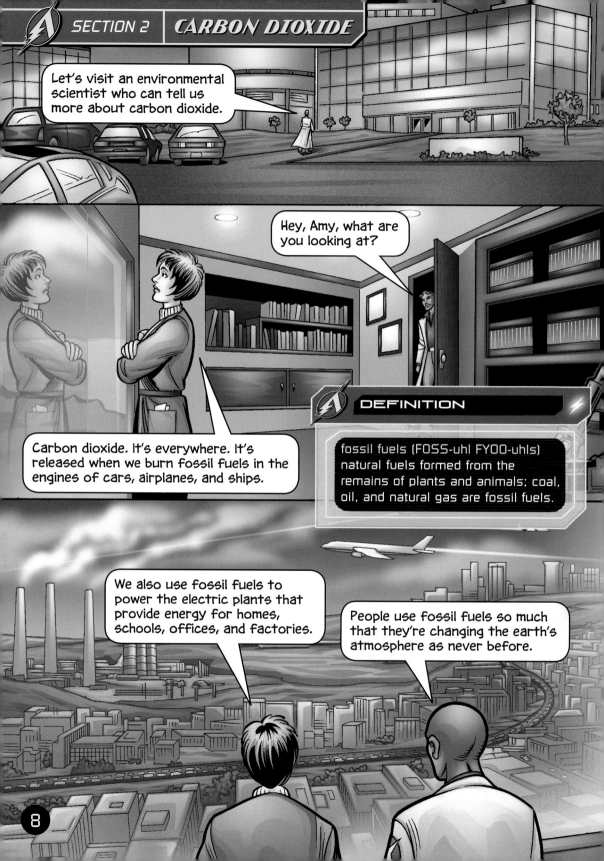

Trees, plants, and even the oceans help take up extra carbon dioxide from the atmosphere.

But in many places, such as the rain forests of South America, people are clearing the forests for farmland.

⚡ DEFINITION

deforestation (di-for-uh-STAY-shuhn)
the clearing of forests by cutting or burning trees

Trees that are burned or left to decompose release carbon dioxide into the air.

Because these dead trees no longer take in carbon dioxide, the buildup of greenhouse gases increases.

WHITE EAGLE SCHOOL LMC

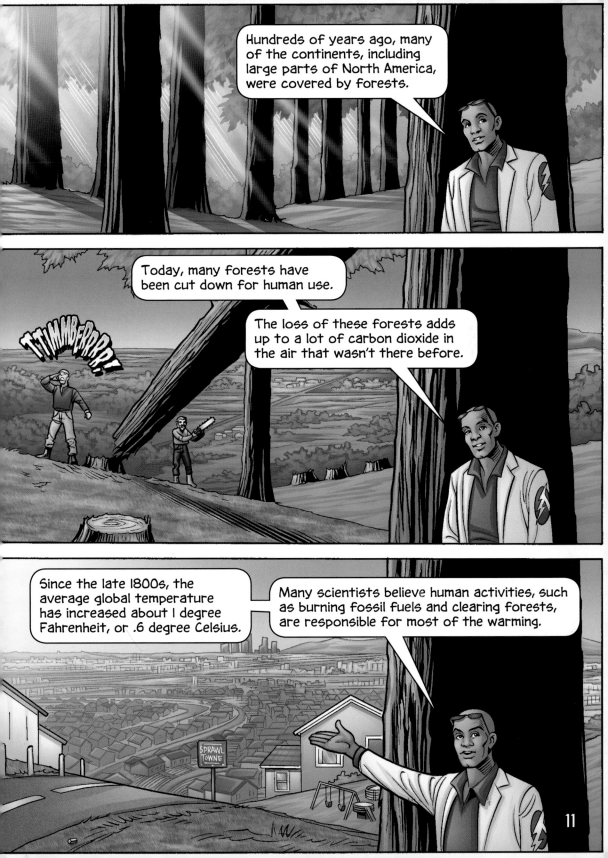

Experts use computer programs to predict how extra greenhouse gases may change the earth in the future.

They predict the average global temperature will rise 2 to 10 degrees Fahrenheit, or 1.1 to 5.6 degrees Celsius, by 2100. This warming could lead to major changes for the planet.

For example, scientists worry about what global warming will do to earth's weather and climate.

SALE up to 50%

BOING

Weather describes the current state of the atmosphere, such as sunny and warm . . .

. . . or cold, rainy, and windy.

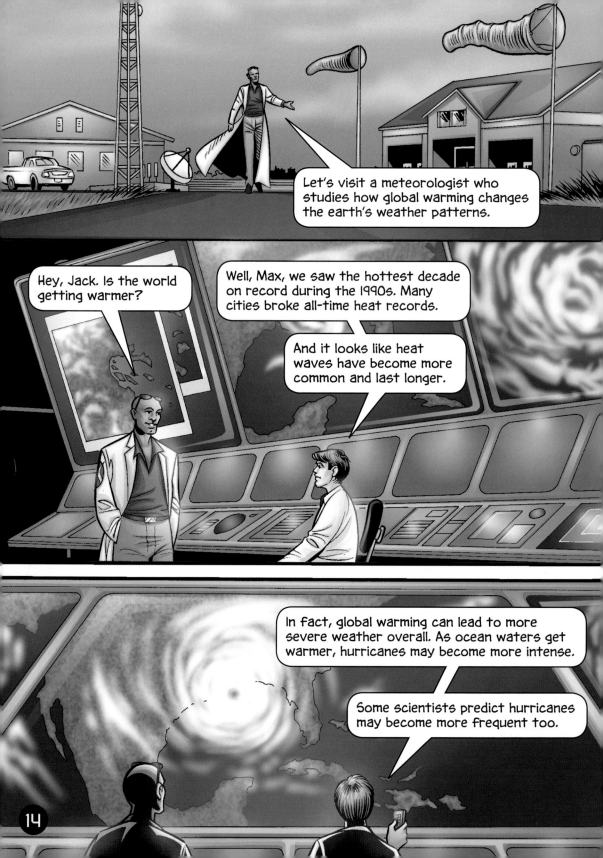

Glaciers are slow-moving sheets of ice and snow.
They show us the impact of global warming because as the world heats up, they melt down.
Already, warmer temperatures are melting almost all of the world's mountain glaciers.
About 150 years ago, the huge Rhone Glacier filled this mountain valley in Switzerland's Alps.
Today, the glacier is nearly out of sight.

But mountain glaciers and ice caps aren't the only large ice masses affected by global warming.

Below me, Greenland's huge ice sheet is also melting faster than expected.

If it ever melts completely, sea levels around the world could rise about 20 feet, or 6 meters. Coastal cities and small island nations would be under water. Millions of people would be forced from their homes.

COASTLINES TODAY

FLORIDA

SOUTHEAST ASIA

COASTLINES IF GREENLAND'S ICE SHEET MELTED

FLORIDA

SOUTHEAST ASIA

But global warming affects more than just humans. It will change animal and plant habitats too.
In fact, many species will have difficulty surviving in the regions where they now live.
Global warming changes habitats faster than plants and animals can adapt.
For instance, polar bears may go extinct if temperatures keep rising. Their hunting grounds are shrinking as the arctic ice melts away.

Plants may be most vulnerable to rising temperatures. They can't move to other habitats like animals can.

For example, the famous fall colors of sugar maple trees in the northeastern United States may become a thing of the past.

These beautiful trees need cooler temperatures to survive. They'll die out as global warming creates longer, warmer summers in this region.

## AGRICULTURAL IMPACT

ACCESS GRANTED: MAX AXIOM

Global warming may benefit some colder regions such as Canada and Russia by creating a longer season to grow crops. At the same time, rising temperatures and droughts may destroy crops in warmer regions farther south.

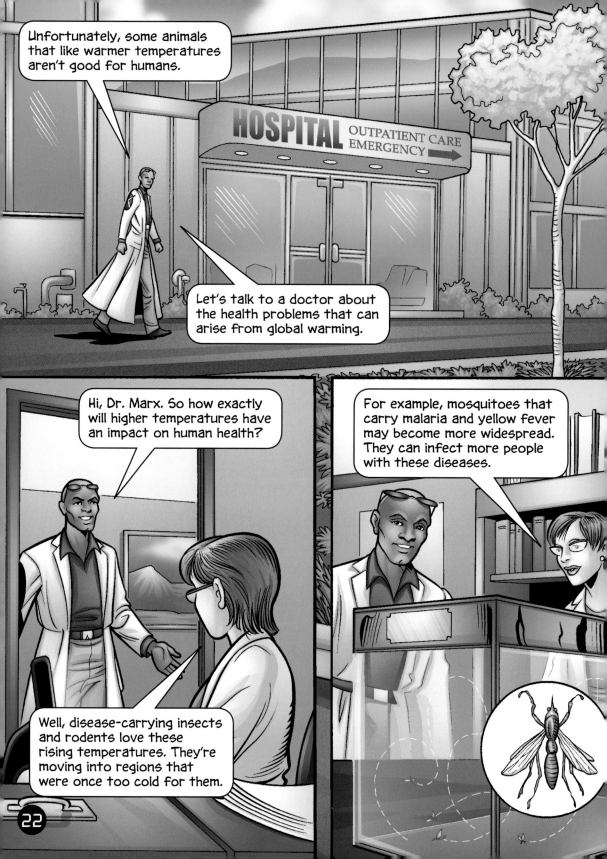

Global warming is a serious issue, but we can find solutions for our environmental problems.

For example, for many years, gases called chlorofluorocarbons, or CFCs, were used as coolants in freezers and air conditioners.

By the 1980s, scientists had discovered that CFCs were thinning the ozone layer high in the earth's atmosphere.

THINNING OZONE LAYER

Because the ozone layer helps block the sun's harmful ultraviolet rays, people worked together to protect it.

By the 1990s, many countries had agreed to stop using CFCs. Scientists expect the ozone layer to recover around 2065.

Turn off appliances and computers if you're not using them.
KLIK
Saving electricity will help reduce the amount of greenhouse gases released into the atmosphere.
And most important, learn more about the environment and tell people what you learn.
Working together we can take positive steps toward solving the problem of global warming.

# MORE ABOUT GLOBAL WARMING

Venus is the hottest planet in our solar system. Many astronomers believe its heat is due to a massive greenhouse effect. Carbon dioxide makes up a whopping 97 percent of Venus's atmosphere. The planet's thick clouds and dense atmosphere help trap the sun's heat, making Venus's surface temperature 870 degrees Fahrenheit (466 degrees Celsius). That's hot enough to melt lead!

After carbon dioxide, methane is the greenhouse gas most produced by humans. Methane is released by landfills and is a by-product of coal mining. Believe it or not, cows are also a source of methane. When cows burp or pass gas, they release methane. As the demand for beef rises, more cattle are raised and more methane is released into the air.

The United States is responsible for more greenhouse gas pollution than any other country in the world.

Hurricanes have different names depending on where they occur in the world. If they appear on the Pacific Ocean, they're called typhoons. When they form on the Indian Ocean, they're called tropical cyclones.

Ozone gas can be good or bad, depending on where it lies in the atmosphere. The ozone layer 10 to 30 miles (16 to 48 kilometers) high works as a shield to protect life on earth from the sun's dangerous ultraviolet radiation. This radiation can lead to skin cancer in humans. Nearer the earth's surface, ground-level ozone is a health hazard, damaging lungs and hurting plants.

The Arctic's sea ice is also melting quickly. Because snow and ice are white, the sea ice works like a big mirror, reflecting most of the sun's rays. As global temperatures rise, however, some of the ice melts. This melting reveals the ocean water below. Because the water is darker than the ice, it absorbs more of the sun's energy and warms up. The warmer water leads to even more of the sea ice melting, which leads to even more water being revealed. The cycle goes on and on.

You've probably seen hybrid cars on the road or on TV. Maybe your family even has one. Hybrid cars run on both gasoline and electricity. Because they don't use as much gas as regular cars, they produce less pollution.

## MORE ABOUT

### SUPER SCIENTIST

**Real name:** Maxwell J. Axiom
**Hometown:** Seattle, Washington
**Height:** 6' 1"      **Weight:** 192 lbs
**Eyes:** Brown      **Hair:** None

**Super capabilities:** Super intelligence; able to shrink to the size of an atom; sunglasses give x-ray vision; lab coat allows for travel through time and space.

**Origin:** Since birth, Max Axiom seemed destined for greatness. His mother, a marine biologist, taught her son about the mysteries of the sea. His father, a nuclear physicist and volunteer park ranger, schooled Max on the wonders of earth and sky.

One day on a wilderness hike, a megacharged lightning bolt struck Max with blinding fury. When he awoke, Max discovered a newfound energy and set out to learn as much about science as possible. He traveled the globe earning degrees in every aspect of the field. Upon his return, he was ready to share his knowledge and new identity with the world. He had become Max Axiom, Super Scientist.

# Glossary

atmosphere (AT-muhs-fihr)—the mixture of gases that surrounds the earth

average (AV-uh-rij)—a common amount of something; an average amount is found by adding figures together and dividing by the number of figures.

carbon dioxide (KAHR-buhn dye-AHK-side)—a colorless, odorless gas that people and animals breathe out; plants take in carbon dioxide because they need it to live.

climate (KLEYE-mit)—the usual weather that occurs in a place

drought (DROUT)—a long period of weather with little or no rainfall

fossil fuels (FOSS-uhl FYOO-uhls)—natural fuels formed from the remains of plants and animals; coal, oil, and natural gas are fossil fuels.

glacier (GLAY-shur)—a huge moving body of ice found in mountain valleys or polar regions

habitat (HAB-uh-tat)—the natural place and conditions in which a plant or animal lives

ozone layer (OH-zohn LAY-ur)—the thin layer of ozone high above the earth's surface that blocks out some of the sun's harmful rays

photosynthesis (foh-toh-SIN-thuh-sis)—the process by which plant cells use energy from the sun to combine carbon dioxide, water, and minerals to make food for plant growth; photosynthesis releases oxygen into the atmosphere.

radiate (RAY-dee-ate)—to give off energy

## READ MORE

Cheel, Richard. *Global Warming Alert!* Disaster Alert! New York: Crabtree, 2007.

Farrar, Amy. *Global Warming.* Essential Viewpoints. Edina, Minn.: ABDO, 2008.

Kowalski, Kathiann M. *Global Warming.* Open for Debate. New York: Benchmark Books, 2004.

Morgan, Sally. *From Windmills to Hydrogen Fuel Cells: Discovering Alternative Energy.* Chain Reactions. Chicago: Heinemann, 2007.

Morris, Neil. *Global Warming.* What If We Do Nothing? Milwaukee: World Almanac Library, 2007.

## INTERNET SITES

FactHound offers a safe, fun way to find Internet sites related to this book. All of the sites on FactHound have been researched by our staff.

Here's how:
1. Visit *www.facthound.com*
2. Choose your grade level.
3. Type in this book ID **1429601396** for age-appropriate sites. You may also browse subjects by clicking on letters, or by clicking on pictures and words.
4. Click on the **Fetch It** button.

**FactHound will fetch the best sites for you!**

# INDEX